LITTLE BITS OF LOVE

ELIZABETH KATIE

SPARK THE BEAT

Edited by Nicole Fegan

Artwork © 2022 by Marisa Paolillo

Copyright © 2021 by Elizabeth Katie

All rights reserved.

No part of this book may be reproduced in any form or by any electronic or mechanical means, including information storage and retrieval systems, without written permission from the author, except for the use of brief quotations in a book review.

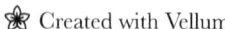 Created with Vellum

I dedicate this book to:

my mother, Sammi, Nick, my NYC foundation and support system, and my Nashville crew—

*Thank you for being a safe place for me,
Always.*

TABLE OF CONTENTS

Note To Readers	ix
Lens of Love	1
1. Romantic Love	2
Lessons I've Learned In Romantic Love	4
Where Do I Begin?	5
You	6
Vulnerable	7
When You Get Me	8
Interlude I	10
I Wish I Could Carry Your Burden	11
Denial	14
What I Want	15
You Make Me Hopeful	16
Pain	17
The Thinker	18
Forgive Me	19
12.16.19	20
What I Had Hoped To Tell You	21
Goodbye	22
I Drank A Lot Of Coffee My First Year in Nashville	23
We're… Friends?	24
The Night I Was Free	25
Aftershock	28
You're Back Again	29
27	30
Midnight Champagne & Page 28	31
Love	34
Old Poems, New Perspective	35
If You Had Let Me	37

Emotional Versus Physical	38
D.	40
You	42
The Future	44
2. Platonic Soulmates & A Mother's Love	45
Lessons I've Learned In This Kind Of Love	46
S.E.A	47
Little Bits Of I Love You	48
On the Living Room Pull-out	50
Sundays Are Keeping Us Alive	52
In Between	54
Mom	57
Little Bits Of Wisdom from my Mother	58
The Little Hyundai Sonata That Could	59
Little Bits of the Worst of Me	61
To My Friends	63
M	64
Friends	67
3. Love Of the Intangible: Places, Phrases, and Passions	68
Lessons In Love You Can't Hold	69
Europe 1	70
Always Back to Brooklyn	71
Aruba	74
Homesick	75
Moving Here Was Tougher Than I Give Myself Credit For	77
Nashville	78
First Weekend Back in NYC	79
Footsteps in the Hall	80
To The Ones I Love	81
Pandemic	82
Wakonda	83
Foreign Language	84
I Wish There Were Words For These Feelings	85
Adventures	86

Little Bits Of Goodbye	87
4. Love Of Me	88
Life Lessons	91
Mantra	92
Me	93
Little Bits Of Contradictions	94
One More Perfect Moment Together	96
2020	97
Choices	99
Between You & Me	100
Safe Love	104
Dreams	108
When It Ends	109
Presence	111
Thank You	112

Note To Readers

Dear Readers,

I made a choice to write this book the way I did instead of writing it in chronological order. While some of the sections do contain pieces of linear storytelling, many do not. Taking it out of chronological order means that you, the reader, will lose some context. But it also means that I can challenge the way you think about different kinds of love.

Please remember some of these poems were written long ago and some for this book. Some are pieces of older poems, taken and shaped and added to, and turned into something new, so that they are still as viscerally real for me today. Some of these poems were cut and reshaped and revised. Some of the poems will mean something different to me years from now. Whatever it means to you, I send it with love.

Love,
    E

Lens Of Love

The truth is that the world is full of beauty.
Love does not change the contents of the picture,
Merely the location and size of the frame.

1. Romantic Love

I hope that when you fall in love, it's the kind of love that makes you learn about yourself. When they tell you they love the mischievous grin you get when you're trying to surprise them, I hope that you learn to appreciate that about yourself, too. I hope it's a love that opens your eyes to the parts of yourself you judged too harshly or skipped over.

I was as close to falling in love as one can get without having ever been with that person. That was my first time ever being in love, if you would call it that. My heart felt like Silly Putty and my idea of what unconditional love was, had been flipped upside down. Love, I realized, takes your heart, with all it has to give, and slowly shows you that your heart can grow bigger, adapt, strengthen. New love doesn't replace the work of the hands that molded it before. Instead, it adds to what you already hold, and reveals that your heart is capable of so much more.

Love is believing that your hope will become reality; that one day you'll utter a question and hear the answer you want. But what takes the place of that answer? Of the answer to a question we haven't yet asked? Fear. If we believe this, then love and fear must be intertwined. Bravery is asking the question anyway.

As you dare to ask each question, your heart bends and shapes and grows to be able to endure whatever is whispered back. Your heart can withstand breaks. And when love is the answer, then it is the answer sung, in a melody more beautiful and harmonious than you could have imagined; the song will bring you home. So be brave. Each time the song fills you, you hold a little more love and a little less fear.

I wrote my friends a letter, to fill them in on my journey

with unrequited love. The trip had lasted about two years. I was in the process of moving on, I was in pain, and I remarked to them, "I know men have fought wars for women they loved. The greatest love songs are about being in love, and people have suffered far greater losses and tragedies than I for having one unrequited love. People are heartbroken and fall out of love all the time. I am under no illusion that, in the scheme of my life, this will be more than a mark, an important time, but I'm starting to think the world is full of people who settle because the person that loves them the most stays silent."

I hope the people I love know how much they matter and know how much they matter to me. I do my best to let them know. But some words are hard to say, and these poems represent the cracks in the foundation I've laid. They are the words that I never got around to saying; they are the questions I never asked. They are for the moments I stayed silent.

Lessons I've Learned In Romantic Love

1. The words we don't say will bury us.

2. It's never as simple as your memory makes it out to be.

3. Some people teach us how to love. Some people teach us how to be loved. If you're really lucky, you'll end up with someone that teaches you both.

4. Society tries to dictate when and who you should kiss, fall in love with, and let into your bed. Live on your own timeline.

5. Don't do anything for the wrong reasons. It's just not that important. It's especially not as important as knowing your own heart, your own skin, your own capacity for love.

Where Do I Begin?

Just begin
I thought,
As if I could just begin to tell the story of you

You

You are a light that dances
And honestly, in a world like this,
You might not even know how magical that is

Vulnerable

I opened myself just a little,
Hoping you'd find your way.
It was just like digging a hole
Out of the sand by the water's edge
With the hope that the ocean
Would fill in the empty spaces;
Just like that,
I didn't know how else to let you in.

When You Get Me

When you get me,
You'll get hesitation.
As we make our way,
Slowly, I won't ever stop,
Noticing the wonder
Of each tiny moment.

When you get me,
You'll get curiosity
As to what comes next,
As well as fear
As to what comes later,
But I will fight for you forever.

When you get me,
You'll get someone
So stubborn,
Both in their ways and
In their love for you.

And when you get me,
You'll have to deal with
Scars I've earned,
But I will make yours
Feel as beautiful
As I think they are—
As you really are.

You'll realize
You're talking about work,
I wasn't listening;
I was noticing the way

Your hand curls
Around your mouth as you speak,
Like your feet by my feet
As we lay.
I will notice
The way the words
Fall from your heart.

I will know
To take your hand—

Often,
I will be restless, anxious,
And I will not remember
Where we're going out to,
Only that it's your mother's birthday
And you'll need ice cream
On the way home,
Because it'll have been too much.
And, I will get it for you
Because if you get me,
Then I get you, too.

Interlude

I'm not sure if writers were meant to love the "right" way, if there is such a thing as a "right" way. I believe many writers spend time trying to notice the unnoticed and distract themselves from a firm reality. I think many writers fall in love with ideas more than anything else. But I also think, because of this, they can see people differently; they will show you a light you emit, where you once thought there was only darkness.

I Wish I Could Carry Your Burden

I wish I could slow time
So that you could fill your days
With good books & warm socks,
With your hand
Curled
Around your mug
& your cat at your feet.
You wouldn't have to worry
About making it on time,
Because time would be
What you had most of.
I wish that I could build you walls
That always stood and withstood,
So that they would keep
You from ever thinking
You didn't have the place
I know you should,
Know what it feels like
To have a place that's not just home,
It's so safe you can feel it in your soul.
Everyone around you is safe too,
And you can just be.
I wish, when you were ready,
That place would be easy for you to find.
In truth,
I've been where you are too.
The scars you see
When you see me
Are from concrete sidewalks,
Forgotten daydreams,
& shattered illusions.

Maybe they make me seem
Like I'm a mess to you,
But I couldn't see
Myself without them anymore.
I wouldn't have found the
Hands that would hold me
Through the moments
That put me back together,
The ones that showed me
Another day comes,
And there's a ground on which
To build upon—
Without them,
Look at all the places
I would have missed
And poetry that would mean so much less.
Some of us don't attract easy,
But look at you;
You make being tough
Look damn easy.
I wish I could show you
Yourself through my eyes
So that you would find them impossible
To open in darkness,
For you had seen so much light.
I wish you would be forever warm,
Never worn out,
And be so sure of yourself
That the light would take the place of your shadow
While you were dancing on worn out streets,
Coming alive, I think
I want to hold your burden for a while,
So that you may feel free
And I could see you drift
With the easiness and loveliness of the world.

I wish I could carry your burden,
So you could just keep dancing forever.

Denial

Sometimes, I think
It's all in your head, you don't really want this,
This is how you feel about a friend.
And then I'm sitting across from you,
Looking at your rolled up sleeves and falling
    down hair
And I think, God, you're sexy.

What I Want

I want to wake up,
My arms around you,
And smile into the t-shirt
That's hanging off your shoulders
So that the first thing you feel
Each morning is the grin that tells you
How happy I am to wake up with you.
I want to wake up with you;
I've never wanted that with anyone before.

You Make Me Hopeful

Once in a while,
I convince myself
Your eyes are lighting up at me,
That it's me you're smiling at,
That mine is the face you're looking for,
The ear you want to hold
Even in a crowd
Because you know I've got you
And I always will.

Pain

Loving you was like releasing the pressure on a
    wound I thought had healed,
Only to find my new white tee covered in blood.
I suppose I could stop the flow, but I was filled just
    as much with wonder as I was with dislike.
I suppose the only thing stronger than instinct is
    love anyway.
The only reason we would put ourselves in harm's
    way is love.
The only reason we sacrifice is love.
I might as well just admit it now; I would bleed dry
    for you.

The Thinker

I felt strangled.
I stood where you had once stood
With so many thoughts and questions.
How many times had your feet stepped here,
Tangled with the dirt underneath?
How many times did you laugh here,
Did you cry here?
Did you study in the shadow of the art
You had brought back to life
While dreaming of what your future would be?
Did it look like now?
Did you clear your mind here?
Were you happy here?
Did a date walk you home
Through these blades of grass
And lean in, to share a kiss with you, right here?
How could I love you so much now
But not be able to know you then?
What was I doing,
Listening to,
While your date was listening
To your laughter
As it reached the open sky?
I want to reach
The part of you that existed
Before our worlds collided,
Before I was strangled,
Trying to make you all my best memories.

Forgive Me

I wish you understood
That disappointing you hurts me,
But it's not nearly as bad
As the pain that would kill me
To fall in and out of love with you again.

12.16.19

I disentangled myself from you,
Branch by branch,
Limb by limb,
City by city.
I moved to forget you,
But now here we are,
Breathing the same air.

What I Had Hoped To Tell You

I had these moments
Where I so desperately wished
It was my place to tell you
How much you deserved to be cherished,
But I never got to,
So I will now—

I hope you're cherished by the sun
And it warms your skin,
Even in the winter months;
I hope you're cherished by the stars
That race to keep up with the light you emit
    through the darkness.
I hope you know that every part of you deserves to
    be recognized
And made to feel as beautiful as I know it to be.
I wish I could have shown you with my hands, my
    mouth;
I wish I could have said these words to you out
    loud.
I hope someone gives you the knowledge of your
    beauty often;
I hope the ones that love you give you at least this
    much.
And I hope you know you won't ever stop being
    beautiful to me.

Goodbye

Let her go.
Let her laugh go as you breathe
In and out, the ocean air
Let it echo through the mountains.
Let the sound of her voice go
In the crowds on the streets
Of a new city
Until it is hidden beneath strangers' voices.
Let the way you feel about her go
In the sound of a celebration on foreign shores.
Leave her behind with every footstep
As you move up the coast.
Leave the parts of her you love—
Piece by piece,
Place by place—
Until it's impossible to put her
Together again,
And you can let her go.

I Drank A Lot Of Coffee My First Year in Nashville

You and I,
I thought to myself,
While sitting with a cup
That I was mad at for being empty
Because I couldn't swirl the coffee and use it to
    distract myself,
You and I,
Are about to do the hard work;
We're going to break open,
And then I hope we'll be okay.

We're... Friends?

I think we may be overcorrecting
You said, in the way that you say things—
Slowly, not quite sure
If the words tumbling out of your lips
Are the words that you want to say—
You're frustrated at yourself.
I doubt I'm helping much.
Am I right?
You asked while you looked at me,
Using your hands to show me
We go this way
And then that way
And eventually,
We'll find our way.
I'm not quite sure what I said back to you in the car,
But those words haven't left me since,
Because you and I
Are always overcorrecting

The Night I Was Free

I keep going back
To that moment in the bathroom.
I remember
Your lips on my lips
And my hands on either side of your face,
My arms
Draped
Over your leg
And the way we were.
I keep going back
To that moment in the bathroom.

I remember the night on replay
And the next days
When I wanted to kiss you again.
You didn't want me in that way,
But you couldn't really
Say it in words,
Because we were too complicated,
Too much a part of each other,
Our lives so intertwined,
As close as two people could be
Without
Being
Each
Other's
Everything.
And I knew it wasn't our time.

Years from now,
It would all make sense.
I could see past us, even then.

But, every once and a while,
The thought would cross my mind
And I would go back to that moment in the
 bathroom.
I went back over and over and over again.
You wanted to take me home;
You wanted me,
And I enjoyed being wanted,
And I wasn't thinking.
Nobody was thinking.
We'd had too much to drink,
And I distinctly recall
Pulling away and
Sending a messenger for our friends,
Who were lost somewhere on the dance floor.
I remember I said
To have them meet me in the bathroom.

And there the three of us were
In the corner stall
In the back of a bar
In the middle of Nashville.
I couldn't know it, but right then
A group of strangers was trying to convince you,
That you had me.

I wonder what you were saying to them
As I was laying out to our friends the two options.
You were so tired.
I could just go
Call you a cab,
Put you in it,
Send you alone,
Or I could go with you.

I forget most
Of what any of us said,
But I still hear her voice,
Like an echo of my conscience saying
You're not ready yet.
And she said it
To let me know
That was okay.

Some part of me
Beyond thinking and reason agreed.
I mean…I wasn't ready yet…but for what?
For you, for more, for what it meant?

It doesn't really matter anymore.

I said goodbye and I put you in the cab.

Every time I start to wonder
What I'm really feeling,
If we're doing the right thing,
Who we'll be to each other in the end,
I go back to the moment in the bathroom
When I could have had you,
But instead,
I let you go.

Aftershock

I don't know if I've ever felt so loved, you said
At least not like that, at least not in a long time.
But you didn't remember the words I had
    whispered, just the way it made you feel
And so it was just another missing piece, for both
    of us.

I wonder how different things would be,
If either of us could recall what was said.
But I think we weren't meant to.

You're Back Again

Why did thoughts of you have to haunt me here?
You could have had anywhere; any city could have
 been yours.
I would have even given you Amsterdam…
On second thought, you can't have Amsterdam.
But it's not like I went and ruined San Francisco
 for you.
Why'd my love for you have to visit me in
 Nashville?

27

Last night made me wonder
What other strangers
Will turn into friends
After we both show our worst moves on the dance
 floor.
What an amazing night,
To show that there is even more to me than I
 know yet

Midnight Champagne & Page 28

I don't know
Who we'll be to each other
In five years,
Ten years down the line,
But I know that right now,
You make me feel a little less alone.

I know I get to be here for all of these
Just-for-me moments:
The first time we drove into a strange
    neighborhood in Nashville,
The concerts in our living rooms,
The 10-hour video shoot that ended in milkshakes
And pictures of you only I could get
Because you were so yourself with me.

There are successes that feel big now
That will one day seem so small;
The moment the crowd hit different
And we took shots of whiskey,
Your joy at hearing your song on Radio SoBro,
And all the days in between.
That walk that we took down Cedar Lane,
A street so full of wonder, I went back just to get
    the name.
Do you remember the hidden gardens, old cars and
    rickety sidewalks it held?
So full of secrets,
I think we fell
In and out of another period of time as we walked.
I think we fell
In and out of love,

During every movie night;
Do you remember the one you chose
Without realizing it was in French
But by the end it had ripped both of our hearts out
    of our chests?
I'm still a little bit mad at you about it.
And let's not forget
The night I turned on The Little Prince
And watched you fall asleep on Zoom,
But I forgave you,
Because you had worked all day and still wanted to
    come through
For me,
For me,
Always for me,
Except you crying at What a Girl Wants
Was a little bit for you.

Hours before your first album released,
I was laying in the park
And I thought,
Damn I have so much
That means so much to me
And hopefully, tonight,
I can just enjoy it all.
Hopefully, tonight
We can just be happy,
And that night we were happy.
From six feet away
We popped champagne
At midnight on your front lawn
And listened to our songs.
We talked about our feelings,
We hugged for the first time in three months,
And I fell asleep smiling because of that hug

And weeks later when you played live for the first time on the radio,
We smoked a little, laughed a little, ate a little too much.
You wanted to take scooters back to my place to celebrate;
You wanted to be there for something I had never done
And as I accelerated and you slowed down
Right before I fell and hit the ground—
Way before we noticed all the blood
And you put hydrogen peroxide on my knee—
Yeah, before that,
I noticed your white tee shirt blowing in the wind in front of me;
I thought about the perfect day we were having
And I asked myself how many times do we need to find magic together
Before I realize the magic is you?

Love

Isn't it funny,
How we stopped putting the I first,
When we say, love you
Now that we're both aware
We might actually mean what we say

Old Poems, New Perspective

"It's felt good before but…
This was like being kissed really well for the first time.
This was like having a smoke but doing it while sitting over the canals of Amsterdam."

I wrote that years before,
And now, years later,
We're on my floor,
Talking about nights out
And boys that we danced with,
That we've kissed, that we want to kiss,
But really we're talking about
What it's like to start to learn ourselves
In the context of here and now.
We're talking about growth and healing
And I'm feeling good
About whatever happened

My old words come back to me
Like a pair of worn-out jeans
I just found in the closet
And I pull them on
But I don't see them in quite the same way anymore.
Now I say,
I've been high in Amsterdam
But I've never felt like this

I'm surprised at my words;
I start to think,
Do I mean that?

Then I find myself going back,
To the canal
Where my sister and I sat
When I had asked
If it was possible to die from happiness
Because I was that happy and a little high

It's only now I know
The boundaries of happiness grow as you grow,
So that happiness you feel when you're
A little healthier, a little stronger
Is different than the happiness you held way back
    when.
One is no more important than the other.

Maybe I've only just touched the edge
Of how good it can get,

It is, it turns out,
All just about a feeling
A feeling that can't be found
Just because I want to find it

I really hope I deserve more of that feeling

If You Had Let Me

I'm back in New York
And thinking of you,
As if I needed an excuse.

I'd like to think that from now on,
I will only love with intention.
I will choose where to put my time and energy,
    carefully
So that even if the feeling doesn't last,
I will know it was worth it to let myself fall.

I fell for you by accident—you were so unexpected
And you didn't love me back,
But I would have chosen to put in the work.
I would have chosen you,
I would have loved you, forever, on purpose.

Emotional Versus Physical

I wonder why those that I've loved the most
Are the same ones I've never gotten to touch or hold.
I've never gotten to lie down next to them
And just kiss them because I wanted to;
They were much too complicated for that;
I wanted them anyway.

What would it have been like
To have loved them and had them love me back?

Still, each taught me more
Than any hands I have held,
Lips that mine have brushed,
Or weekend I have spent sharing myself intimately by touch.

I think of all the people
Who can so easily take someone home
But have no one to call
At 3 a.m. to talk about their feelings with,
Or to pick them up when they have a flat tire.
This whole time I've been bitter;
It's so hard for me to be casual about taking someone home,
But I seem to have forgotten that I have so many people to call
At 3 am to talk about my feelings with
Or to pick me up because I have a flat.

One day I want to know
What it's like to love someone

Who loves you the same way in return
And have it just be that simple.

But first,
I want to go on a date—
The type they sing about in country songs.
And I want to kiss a stranger with ginger hair,
And I hope I get to feel passion,
The kind of attraction
That stops me from thinking.
I just want to keep kissing,
No, I need to, as their lips give me permission—
To want them that badly.

I want to run into that cute stranger I met at the park,
The one where I got the dog's name but forgot to ask him for his,
And ask him for his.

I hope I kiss men and women and fall
Into bed and out of lust
And along the way
I hope I can appreciate
That my body and my heart and my mind
All took a while to catch up to cach other.

D.

Sometimes you hold me in your arms
And I think I might be falling in love with you.
Other days I think about how good I am on
    my own,
And the things I want that I won't be able get with
You, talk about me loving you in the short term
Like you can feel my rumination in your bones,
And it breaks my heart
Because I'm happy here with you
But we both know, I'll never be satisfied.
Five years from now,
You'll probably be shirtless
On the cover of some magazine—
All the girls will want you, and I'll think,
I had him—had you—in unbuttoned jeans.
After you had me, I put back on my tee,
And we sat half-naked on my couch,
With Folklore playing in the background
And I take a moment not to look around
But just to look at you like that,
Cause I like the way your body looks in the shadow
    of the light.
And we're just waiting on this high to kick in—has
    it kicked in?
When will this food arrive?
Then I start to say words that sound like…
You look so, wow, and I'm telling you how
You'll look just like this on the cover of GQ
    one day,
And all the girls will want you, but you just kiss me
    and say
I'm happy right now and that's all that matters.

What a gift to learn from you about being in the present
I'm thinking about where I'll end up and who I'll end up with
And you're so unconcerned with anything other than holding me.
I think you'll make me a better me if I can just let myself live
The experience I'm sad about losing one day.

You

You came out of nowhere.
You entered as a little ball of energy
And announced your existence in my chest.
And yet, I still don't know who you are,
But I can feel you getting closer,
And I know you will change my life.

Sometimes I get in my head
About love and lust and life
And I'll pull myself back into this feeling in me,
That says you're coming.

When I'm in it, I feel…at peace,
Calm and warm and so sure,
Like I'm wrapped up with you already, and…
And wait, am I crazy?
Are you real?
You feel real.
I already know you're so beautiful,
Nothing I've ever seen could compete,
And you are gonna make me laugh like nobody else
And you'll be kind, and honest, and vulnerable,
    and spiritual,
And my appreciation of you will need to burst out
    of my bones,
And you'll love this poem,
And you'll love me,
And you'll make me more…me,
For however long I get to hold you.
But I think before you,
I'm going to have quite a year—
A year full of good love and good sex,

That was grown from friendship
And turned into, passionate experiments.
And there will be a lot of adventure,
All to prove to myself
That none of it satisfies me
In the way I expect it not to.

But when I finally accept that,
Right after I take a big deep breath in,
There will be you.

The Future

Maybe I was wrong;
Maybe it's him

2. Platonic Soulmates & A Mother's Love

If I were never to be lucky again, I'd still consider myself far luckier than I deserve. If you knew the people in my life, you would understand why.

It wasn't always easy for me to make friends, especially good friends. I was different and I was bullied. I was emotionally abused by my own father at home and the choices he made literally tore my already small family apart. I don't have many blood relatives left that I talk to.

But as a result of all of that darkness, I found the most incredible group of people. Whenever someone new comes into our lives and experiences what we have as a group, they always remark about what they've just become a part of. Somehow, we found each other.

I have friends that know I'll always give them my jacket because they are cold so they take theirs off first. I have friends that have shown up on a cold winter day to change a tire for me. I have friends that check in just because, and make sure I get home safe. I have the "if you need to get home in the next day and there are no flights, we'll get in the car together and drive" type of friends.

There is only truth between us—none of that "what you want to hear" bullshit. There's honesty, trust, a lot of laughter, and usually good food.

Lessons I've Learned In This Kind Of Love

1. Love is love for everybody. Love is only love if it is for everybody. Love is only right that way. Besides, the more love in the air, the better.

2. It never gets easier to accept when bad things happen to good people because they don't deserve it. Good people deserve beautiful things.

3. It's not about how many people love you, it's about how much love you receive from the people you do have in your life. It's about good love, deserving love. It's about love earned by being there for someone and having them show up for you too. That's the only love that matters.

4. I want to tell you, each "you," how much you matter. Life is too short to be ashamed.

S.E.A

I hope our hearts beat as one,
While remaining in each of us,
Letting us be together
Even when we are apart

Little Bits Of I Love You

I

This is for the ones
Who know me better than I know myself,
And for every time,
I hated so much, how right you were.

II

I want to look at you,
All of you.
I want to stare so hard
That you're so ingrained
So when we part
The memory lives on
In the wisps of us
Still left in the air.
I want to hear you laugh,
Really laugh,
And feel your heartbeat as you laugh.
I want to feel you
As you are really alive.
Sometimes I wish
You could see you as I do.

III

In the quiet moments with you,
I hear so much beautiful music,
I wonder how people live without your sound.

IV

Lying next to someone you love
Might just be the safest place in the world

On the Living Room Pull-out

I remember the first time I loved
The sound of you snoring.
We had been woken up so early,
By a pounding on the door
With bad news.
We were so tired,
Our eyes kept fighting to stay awake and
I remember finally giving in,
Pulling out the couch,
Laying down,
How we could feel the springs
In our backs.
We were across the mattress from each other
But I could feel the closeness between us;
We were together.
I wanted to reach out and put my arm around you
But didn't want to wake you,
If sleep had already become you.
There you were—my blood,
Keeping me safe.
Surrounded by blankets,
Keeping the cold out,
They felt so good against my skin
And I used them to keep the light out,
Peering around them to look at you,
Making sure you were still there.
I remember I couldn't sleep,
Scared at every sound.
The deep voice outside
Felt raw against my bones;
I wanted it to go away
To drown it out

And suddenly the sound I had always hated
Filled me with love—
You started breathing,
Really breathing,
Deep breathing,
The kind that makes a sound.
And I smiled;
I wanted more.
I tried to make mine sound like yours
You stopped so suddenly, restless,
Moving your head more then you usually do
And the sweet sound of peace was gone
And I thought,
They could take anything
As long as I don't lose you.

Sundays Are Keeping Us Alive

The you I appreciate the most—
Do you know that you?
It's the you that's lying next to me.
That's it, it's that simple.
We could be in Prague on a rainy day in a hotel
    room meant for a couple
Or on the pull-out couch while strangers search our
    house,
And I will still feel safe with you.

I loved Sunday mornings when I would crawl into
    your bed and we would both lie there
    peacefully,
Not really speaking.
The sun would come through the window,
And it was the slowest pace you were ever at.

Sunday mornings were what I was scared of losing
    most.

I would lie there,
Lazily watching you breathe,
Listening for the sighs that were really sounds of
    happiness,
I'd enjoy the first taste of a perfect day.

Sunday's were for us to just…be.

Then Sundays turned into me crawling into
    your bed,
And sending Nick to make breakfast,

Cause that spot in the bed was for me first.
And Sundays, you know, are always for good
>breakfast.

In Between

It's not the big days, the birthdays, or the holidays;
I'll be home for those.
It's not the happy hours, the parties, or the work events
I'd attend as your plus one,
It's the moments in between
When I might catch you in passing,
Because I would just be getting home
And you would probably be leaving,
Or I'm going to work
And you're going to sleep.
It's the feeling that if you were here,
We would mix my blackberry iced tea
And your lemonade and make something better
But I'm holding one cup and she's holding another
Because she's not you
And you should be here.
Honestly, you would enjoy this farmer's market
    more than me anyway.

We can have a barbecue together at any time
But suddenly it's the night before the 4th of July
And I'm not making too many Jello shots
While you bake something themed
(It would definitely be themed)
And misshapen
And delicious,
And I'm trying it first.
It kind of hurts,
And it only gets worse
When you say that we can still
Hear each other's words, but it's not the same,

It's your body being here, you tell me
It's just being in each other's presence,
And what can I say?
Because I do miss you
But to be fair,
I only miss you in between,
In between day and night,
In between Sunday and Sunday.
It's not that we're in two cities,
It's the damn 900 miles in between.

It's the stories not big enough for you to tell over the phone
But they made your minute or your day.
Forget the big moments,
What I miss the most
Is the "just because" smile I get to catch,
The before and after activity naps
When your blanket is hanging over your face,
And I think, where is her face?
It's the "we both stop and catch our breath" glances,
Ok—I stop and catch my breath and glance
At you,
As you do,
A workout I'm really not good at.

It's the time we spend together on the commercial breaks
Of the tv show we're watching that we both hate
But just have to finish anyway.

The chatter of our shower conversations,
The silence as I change the song in the car

Cause I want to hear you sing country songs with a
    twang.

I miss the mumbles I give
Right after my eyelids have closed
But right before I sleep,
When I turn my head toward you
So you think that I'm wide awake,
And you hate that.

But it's fine, okay?
I only miss
There being nothing in between you and I
Except an entire lifetime
Pulling us closer
Until we can't be any closer.

I only miss you,
Always
In between.

Mom

I had this theory when I was young
That between band-aids, ketchup, and moms,
You could fix anything.

In many ways, I still believe
All of the above will protect you;
From bad tasting food,
From hurt,
From wounds,
And from the world.
And they add a little flavor while covering up the
 bad parts.

I'll try not to talk about my need
For hypoallergenic adhesives
Or my love for ketchup,
But I can tell you about the journey we took
 together with pasta—
And the time my mom had to go to the store
In the middle of an Italian dinner
To buy me Heinz.

Little Bits Of Wisdom from my Mother

1. Every time you do a hard thing it gets easier. So I do the hard thing if it's the right thing, and it does get easier.

2. If it was the right decision for you at the time, it was the right decision.

3. When I was little and I would get scared, I would ask my mom to promise me that I would be okay. I knew my mother believed the words If she said them, so I believed them too. I want to be that honest. I want to make people feel safe. And I want it to be that easy, to feel safe again.

The Little Hyundai Sonata That Could

The Hyundai was a gift from my Grandmother,
Given to me a little before she wanted to let it go,
And I think the car knew that;
I think that car was always on my grandmother's side.

The visors won't stay up,
Not with velcro or tape,
And if I'm not gentle with it
The glove compartment breaks.
There are leaks that come and go
And the low, low, low,
Rumble from the front end,
That no mechanic can diagnose or mend,
And the sound gets worse every winter still
And there is a low and constant shrill
Coming from the dash, that never stops.
But in the car's defense,
That one might be from the radio my sister and I put in;
Let's not forget the constant flat tire problem,
The summer ant problem
Or how it rains on the inside while I drive –
It drives me, crazy
But it also gave me
A way to drive around Brooklyn
And later on it would take me to Nashville,
From Brooklyn to Nashville,
From Nashville to Brooklyn,
And back again.

On that first drive,

With my mom by my side,
It shook every single time
I accelerated past 70,
But we made it.

Then that car took me around my new city,
Just a little piece of home,
That I had taken with me.
And once or twice, inside
D watched his life flash before his eyes.

It's been at least a million times
That the car has had concerts in it,
Loved ones in it,
I used to try to beat my sister home in it,
And way back when,
Me and my friends,
Decided it had heard so many secrets and stories
That we would call it Pope Usher,
After the two people in the world we associated with confessions.

At 15 years old, with only 60,000 miles on it,
It has cost more money
Than something new
But it protects me and
I…I miss my grandmother,
So I hold on to the car as if I am holding on to her
And it's just like her—
Tiny, determined, interesting, and a little bit of a mess,
And I love her just the same

Little Bits of the Worst of Me

I

I love my eyes
But I hate that they came from you,
As if they are there to remind me
I have something beautiful in common with a monster.

II

Would you think
The worst parts of me
Were really the worst
If they hadn't come from him?

III

I don't even want what you have,
So why am I jealous?
Perhaps it's the ache to feel
So passionately about something,
Even if what's making you feel that way
Would not make me feel that way.
Perhaps it's just the human in me.
I envy how you can feel
Without thinking about how you might feel,
And how you know what you want
Because you know yourself so well.
And you're confident about it—
Don't even get me started on the confidence.
I'm not sure I have one friend I wasn't at some point intimidated by.

Here I am waiting for my new friends to make it to
 their car
So I can go back and buy something
I thought I wanted in the moment
But didn't get.

To My Friends Part 1

All the best people I know—
The strongest, the smartest, the funniest, the most
    beautiful inside and out,
The ones who on their best days are sure of
    themselves—
Also have these moments of deep insecurity,
When what they need is to hear somebody else
    tell them
That they are all those things I mentioned—
That they are desired,
That they are loved
Despite their imperfections,
And I think that tells you all you need to know
About how there are no absolutes.

To My Friends Part 2

There is space for you to be who you want to be
There is space for you to be who you need to be
There is space for you to be you exactly as you are

To My Friends Part 3

I'm sorry if anyone ever told you
That your being different was exhausting
Or a burden
Or something they couldn't handle.
Your different
Is everything I love about you
And I want more of it

M.

How did you know?

Three or four weeks in,
That we were going to be
What we are for each other…

How did you know?

That when I went back home,
I was going to start to realize
What you had already realized…

How did you know?

You would help bring me back here,
And I would need you,
You would need me—
We would need each other…

How did you know?

That I had room for one more best friend,
That there was more room for my heart to grow,

I think back to when I had just moved in.
We were sitting on my floor,
And you said, I think
We will need you
In ways we don't know yet,
And you will need us,
In ways you don't know yet.
And then you taught me about value

Well, you taught me about a lot of things that I
    thought I already knew,
How…how…how did you know when you said
All of our lives were about to change?
I was just so afraid that that would be true,
And I wanted to stay where we were,
I wanted to hold on a little bit longer.
My feet were just starting to find their way onto
    solid ground,
My fingers were just starting to tangle with the
    edges of happiness;
I had just begun to explore the parts of me
That had been begging me to shine a light on them
And you were helping me shine a light on them,

And I wanted more gluten free baked goods
In the bed of your pickup
And more life changing conversations
Over coffee and pho.
I wanted more of all of us drunk in this apartment,
And writes that turned into talks
That turned into nights that turned into writes,
And I still wanted more of all of it,
Just a little more of the way it was

When the pandemic came.

And you packed up
And left for three months,

You were steady, I was afraid.

Now you are about six hours from getting back to
    Nashville,
We're closer than before,

And I know we will have to say goodbye again too
    soon,
And I won't know how to.

But you will.

You don't know everything,
But you sure know how to help me heal
And move forward,
And you have taught me how to be loved—
How to really accept love—
And I think discovering what's next with you
Is going to be better than what was,
I just don't know how
For once, I don't think you know either.

But being your friend,
And figuring it out,
Has been the greatest adventure.

Other things you knew: How to drive stick, how I felt about him before I did, and how important Scooby Doo nights are.

Friends

I often write poems about friends
That come off as romantic
But I'm done pretending
That I don't feel the way I feel about them—
Somewhere between I love you
And I'm in love with you.

What other words could fully encompass
Wow, you saved my life again and again
And I love you so much just for being you?

3. Love Of the Intangible: Places, Phrases, and Passions

I've fallen madly in love with music. So much so I couldn't possibly put it into words. But I'll try because I'm also in love with words. I'm a word nerd.

I'm in constant love with traveling. God, I hope I never fall out of it. I love getting lost on foreign streets and discovering a new corner of the world with someone I adore.

I was lucky enough to visit Iceland some years back where I spent some time on the top of a glacier. It was, incredible. I looked at the color and openness of the sky and noticed how the world seemed so vast.

Just a few weeks later I found myself back in Brooklyn shoveling snow off the sidewalk. I looked around at how crowded the city seemed. Those moments within a few weeks of each other taught me something very important—that the very experience of something like snow can take on such a different meaning with just a slight change of perspective.

Do you know how beautiful snow becomes when it's not a responsibility or a walking hazard for your neighbors? Context is everything. Traveling takes something ordinary and turns it into something magical; traveling changes your context.

Still, I also love New York City. I have an affection for that city like no other.

I hope you read this section and you also think about the thing or the place that makes you all warm and excited inside. Let others call us weird. What a beautiful thing it is to be moved so deeply by something that can never truly be yours.

Lessons In Love You Can't Hold

1. Live a life that excites you—your excitement matters.

2. Sometimes good things happen slowly, little thing by little thing.

3. Don't forget the bigness of those small moments. Sometimes the small moments are the big ones.

4. Life can be ordinary and magical all at once.

Europe 1

If anything, we are infinitely human—
Nothing to the sand, to the sea, to the stars, to
    the sky

Always Back to Brooklyn

I'd like to believe
My heart first beat
In my mother's womb
In Brooklyn,
And that you can still feel it
Pulsating through the streets,
Mixed with the sound of drummers
On the corners outside of bodegas,
And that sound is calling me home.

I'd like to think the air inside me is a little dirty
Because the air's a little different in New York City;
It's a little dirty,
But I can breathe easier there.

These Converse have been up and down the streets
And all the stairs that lead down to foundations
And back up to the subways in the sky.

There used to be a trace of me on so many
    avenues,
But I'm afraid what was left has been washed away.

There's a parking lot over there
That used to be a diner—our diner;
We went there after prom.

We took our family pictures in Prospect Park
Right over there.

There's a ghost of me on the corner in Park Slope

Where he kissed me right before he got on the
>   train.

There are parts of Central Park
I didn't discover until my late twenties.

I could never show you this place the way I see it
But I could also never claim it to be mine,
With all of its curves and turns,
I could never touch each texture and commit it to
>   memory.

I could eat and eat and eat
And never take in every smell and flavor.

I had a life there.
For 27 years,
I built a life there,
Went from meetings to meeting with friends,
Friends that I still love.
I had dates with boys I don't talk to
And met she who still lingers.
I think of all I tried there, all I experienced there,
Because there's always something new to you in
>   New York.
I tried ax throwing, yoga-boxing, steel drum
>   lessons,
I walked the Highline and got lost in the low lights
>   of dive bars.
Goodbye to Pacific Standard, thank you for what
>   you were.

If you wonder—what's it like to grow up in NYC?
It's a love it and hate it kind of thing.
You love it,

Then sometimes you hate that you love it,
Because it will wear you down if you let it.
Then you go away
And come back,
Land in JFK,
Look around at people
Murmuring with excitement
As they see the city for the first time.
And you think,
This is home,
I'm just home.

Aruba

I like seeing beautiful landscapes
And feeling the luxury of warm ocean waves.
I like starting new books in hidden chairs
Where I can curl up and be cozy
Or swaying in the hammock, lazily lying
With someone I love, worn from nothing but
    the sun.
I like when the chaos of my mind
Meets the calmness of the sea,
And having moments of reflection.
Give me salt water on my tongue before the
Pre-dinner drinks and the taste of
A familiar food cooked in an entirely new way;
Add in too much gelato and good company
Before we wake to a strong cup of coffee
And a sense of adventure.
Let us see something new,
Learn with our hands
And our eyes
And our noses
About things we never learned before.
I fall in love with new places
For all these reasons and more.
I mean there's something to be said
About a trip that was carved out of space and time
With there being nothing to do, no agenda, but
    making memories.

Homesick

Home was…
Complicated
Wonderful
Necessary
For my soul
Hard to settle
1 foot there
1 foot here.
Coming to an understanding,
Joy, amazing birthdays, time with friends,
Living the parts of my life I loved again,
Family, vacations, family vacations
Christmas Eve Eve, a wonderful Christmas, phone calls back to Nash.
Packing, anxiety, uncertainty, excitement, rush, slow, settle, fear,
Try loving what you have,
Car rides, long car rides, "just want to get there" car rides,
Inspections of new places, aching muscles,
Help from friends, we are reunited and falling back into step,
We are falling back into
Writing,
Frustration,
Writing frustration,
Again, again, again,
Homesick,
Rescheduling, let downs, disappointments,
Chances and book clubs,
Dreading work, needing money,

Friends, helping, loss, mom in pain at the loss of
    her sister
Feeling conflicted about where to be,
Good writes, we're not good enough
Sam, I miss your voice
I need you, need you, need, I need
I'm not processing that I have to say goodbye,
That I have to say hello to old goodbyes,
Fighting, new territory, make up, we're in pain
It's raw, real, need, neeeed, need
To hear your voice, whispering to me.

Moving Here Was Tougher Than I Give Myself Credit For

I want home to be the place I need to be,
But sometimes it isn't.
So when life isn't easy here,
I think to myself,
Then go home,
You could have been that version of you back
    there,
But you came here to grow.

Nashville

I'm sure it would have been nice
To have the money
To buy a couch,
But there were so many moments
That I thought,
I think the point of now
Is sitting on the floor
Eating badly-made food
I just attempted to cook,
With nothing around us
But musical instruments,
Tools to create,
And cheap liquor,
We didn't have a bluetooth speaker for the music;
We just made our own.

First Weekend Back in NYC

I look around
Before I close and lock the door
As if this is the last look of the place that I'll
    ever get.
Because even with two homes
I don't know how to go
And come back to a place that's all mine yet.

Footsteps in the Hall

I've been here quite a few months now.
You would think I would be used to the sounds
Of neighbors coming home,
But the noise still makes me tense.

I was never bothered in my dorm room
Or any hotel room
Or the Airbnb where I spent three months in
    Nashville,
But when I close my eyes here,
I'm back in my childhood room
And the footsteps are my mom's
As she gets ready for bed.
Or wait, no,
Maybe it's my sister's instead;
She must be coming home.
And just for a moment
With my eyes closed,
I think if I turn around
The walls will be blue
And my bed will be smaller.

I reach out and touch the boundaries of my new
    place
And it's like I'm stretched out 900 miles away
And when I wake…wait…
Why are there so many voices?
Voices that I don't know,
As I realize where I am
A part of me suddenly aches
To be surrounded by the people I left

To The Ones I Love

I wake and walk the streets of Tennessee.
I think about you,
The ones I love.
I will see you again soon
And I…I cannot wait to hold you.

Pandemic

I liked wandering around a city that was now
    my home
As if I was wandering foreign streets,
Learning where each curve in the road led,
Stumbling upon empty campuses that would
    transport me elsewhere.
I'd get lost and care about flowers,
And I hoped I would never forget
The first taste of that
Medium vanilla iced latte
From Portland Brew
That I sipped in the sun
After almost two months
Of making myself terrible-tasting coffee.
Why does it taste so much better when they put the
    sugar in?

Wakonda

And just for a moment—
Before the first sounds of thunder rolled in
And I ran for my life towards my mother,
Cause I'm still a little bit scarred
From that storm I got stuck in in New Orleans—
Just before that,
I was in the middle of a lake
Looking at the trees covered in the fog that comes
    in with the rain
It was pouring down
The droplets skipped the surface,
And it was hard to tell where it stopped and the
    lake started,
But there was cold and there was warmth.
And I thought damn this is kind of amazing
This is a moment I'll write about later

Foreign Language

I think of friends laughing
As they stumble
On a foreign syllable;
They are learning it for the first time.

I think of the feeling
You get the moment
You learn of a saying
That describes something in a way
You thought you could never explain

I like when words get put together in a way that
    makes your hands tingle.

And I love the way words sound falling off of
    your lips

I Wish There Were Words For These Feelings

Hearing a song you haven't heard in years and singing the words you didn't know you remembered.

Hearing a song you haven't heard in years and feeling what you used to feel when you would hear it.

Finding a place and wondering about the people who found it first.

Experiencing something wonderful with someone you love. Wanting to travel with them, wanting to dance with them. Listening to a song with them and having it travel from your ear to your heart, sparking something within you. Them making you feel safe and at home.

The awareness that you're more alive than you've ever been.

The realization you come to that if you had done one thing differently, you wouldn't be here.

The realization you come to that if you had done one thing differently, you wouldn't be here; to know how loved you are and can be.

Adventures

I want to climb mountains with you.
I want our feet to play along
Foreign shores and when we leave,
We will have to shake sand out of our shoes.
I want to see your eyes light up
The moment you fall in love
With a new city at night.
I want to memorize the way
Your face is carved into the night sky,
Behind you,
The waves lashing
Against the boat we are on.
I want to wake up just a little bit early
While you still rest,
And frame the moment
With the window behind you.
I will feel safe then, content knowing you are too,
And I will wish to stay there forever,
Though I know we have more mountains to climb.

Little Bits Of Goodbye

Moving Away

When I left home.
It was not the hardest thing I ever did—
It was leaving again and again,
Torn apart just a little bit more
Each time I turned away.

The Echo of Goodbye

I'm haunted by goodbyes—
All the ones that have happened,
And all the ones that will.

Nostalgia

Everything and everyone becomes a memory.

Aftermath

Thank God
That just for a moment,
We got to touch normal again.

I now know there is something worth returning for.

4. Love Of Me

I had just made a month-long trip home for the first time in six months. I had never before been away from my family for that long. Going home was…shocking. After everything that transpired before I arrived, I felt a bit broken. I came back to life a little bit at a time. For all of us who have experienced 2020, we have all done so in our own ways. This year, among many other things, I learned how important a good hug can be.

This chapter is not a reflection of the year. It just so happens that many of the topics I talk about were also very present as we experienced the pandemic.

I **fear** the capacity we have inside us. You see, I believe in souls. Sometimes, I like to think of our souls like trees that are planted somewhere deep inside of us. The "trees" start as just a seed. Then it grows as we do, curving and winding along the way. We gain and break branches as we make choices. We bloom as we live well. The roots grow further and further into us until we could not possibly live without this tree; the source of energy that fuels us.

The more we push ourselves, and the more we learn and love, the more we water that tree. The more we do that, the more seeds spring from ourselves and sprout plants elsewhere, in others, with the parts of us we leave in our wake. The more we heal and cut off the rotted branches, the lighter we grow and the more we give the most fulfilling parts of our tree's sun.

But we're not all light. We all have the incredible capacity for both sides of the equation. I tend to really fear the capacity we have for darkness. I try to find the rot before it spreads. But even though we spend time trying to examine every inch, we will never be able to count every grain. There are parts of me I can't reach, can't protect myself from. So, I run.

I'm also really afraid of the ocean; which is perfect for someone whose mother loves the ocean. Don't get me wrong, I love water, but I tend to fear it when I can't see through to the bottom. I also dislike that feeling of being pulled under the waves, probably because it takes me to the bottom.

I know a lot of people fear the ocean, and it's easy to fear; it's dark, filled with mysterious creatures, and there's so much we don't know about it. Am I projecting?

The point is, I think when we finally get to the bottom of the ocean, we'll find out that the place we thought was filled with darkness is really the place where all the light is found.

Maybe we had it wrong the whole time and we've been looking up, at the sun, at the sky, when we should be looking at the bottom of the ocean.

I'm starting to think maybe people are like that too. The darkest parts of ourselves—in our minds, in our soul, the places we hide from—are the ones that need a little more love. Because underneath the "bad" parts are where the best parts are. If we can acknowledge all of ourselves and still choose to keep going, to be good people, to heal and to love, that's bravery. If you see the light at the end of the tunnel, keep going, and live in it as long as you can.

I learned over the past couple of years that accepting that I had been through trauma and accepting that I had been traumatized are two very different things. In 2020, to continue on my journey of healing, I chose words to reflect on throughout the year. Those words were: value, vulnerability, balance, patience, and trust. And this saying: Have faith in what you don't know yet. That saying was to remind me to believe that the unexpected can mean good things are coming too.

I want to do something that I fall madly in **love** with. I want to do something that fulfills me. Challenges me. Allows me to help people. Makes me feel good. I want to learn something new. I want to see the world with people I love. I want to touch the edge of my **dreams**.

The dreamer in me and the part of me that's healing needed space to be heard over the fear and the trauma too. The chapter is messy, as am I.

I hope I end this book where my next steps begin—living in a little bit of light. Thank you for joining me on the journey.

Life Lessons

1. You spend so long getting yourself through something and finding yourself. And by the time you do, your self has changed. And then you start over.

2. If you were waiting for permission to change, like I was at one point, this is it. This is your permission. Go on and grow.

3. We are who we are when the world is not looking.

4. Just because we're not what other people need in the moment doesn't mean we're not enough.

5. It's not easy to be different. Most of us will never win awards for it. And it can be so tempting, just so tempting, to want to take the other way and try and be something you're not, to try and fit in. While your different is beautiful, telling yourself that doesn't make the hard days easier or the long nights shorter. So take as long as you need in order to be okay with you. It's not wasted time. And you are certainly not alone.

6. Patience is giving time and space to a feeling or an experience. Patience is a gift you can give yourself when you are not ready for the next step. **On the other side of patience is possibility.**

7. Sometimes the most important things are everything and nothing all at once.

8. A good hug can change your life.

Mantra

When I'm about to face a fear
I remind myself that at one point
The bravest thing I did in a day
Was to get out of bed
And put two feet on the floor at the same time.
Suddenly, the hard thing seems easy.

Me

There I was,
In a hotel in Seville,
Half-naked on the bed
With an espresso and a chocolate chip cookie,
And no moment represented me more than that—
Full of wonder and full of comfort.

Little Bits Of Contradictions

Afraid

I am made of equal parts wonder and fear,
Which makes for many uncertain adventures.

Free

I breathe in the outside air,
Feel the elements on my face,
Let my eyes graze over you,
And realize as I catch the city through the window,
That there are always boundaries.
Yes, even though I am free to roam,
I am still captive.

Bold

Give me whiskey and jazz, and let me dream.

But Afraid

Who am I to dare to dream?
Who am I to dare to dream
When life is so fragile?

Ready But...

I have the shy demeanor of a poet
But the need for validation like an artist
And the anxiety of both.

Grateful but...

One part of me says,
Look at this beautiful life you have,
Most people live their whole life
And never get this lucky
And the other voice says
So why do I want more?

Because you are human and enough is never
    enough

One More Perfect Moment Together

I wish sometimes that it was easy for me to let
    moments be.
I wish I could let the moments of magic just be.

What if I didn't end a moment
Because I had to be somewhere at some time,
Or out of anxiousness to end it,
While it still feels so good?

I'm sure at some point someone else will change
    the conversation
Or stand up from the bench or the blanket in the
    sand,
Or step away and into the next part of their day,
But I no longer want it to be me.

2020

I rather enjoy my own company
When I'm reading books in the sunshine,
A cold drink by my dangling hand,
Or as I sit typing up novels in coffee shops.

It doesn't scare me to wander through this life
Without knowing if I'll still live alone years
    from now
Because I have so much love from so many
    people—
I am the luckiest that way.

Sometimes during a romantic comedy
Or around couples that are wrapped up in each
    other,
I crave intimacy for a moment,
But never enough to truly change my priorities;
No one knows me the way music knows me.

Sure, I felt a little alone when my family fell apart,
When my mind tore itself to pieces,
And I hit a rock bottom so dark
I thought I would never see the light again,
But here I am,
In the park,
In the middle of a pandemic,
And I'm lonelier than I've ever been.
I'm feeling loneliness so deep within,
I think I understand people better now.

I had never thought that there would be a day
I couldn't just get on a plane

And go home,

But here I am

And I thought about what Mitch had said—
It's the worst Would You Rather, isn't it?
So much time to spend
But so far away from the people you want to spend
    it with.

Yet here I am

Choices

I'm glad I didn't get to choose
My own tragedies and triumphs
Like it was a fill-in-the-blank,
Choose your own adventure story.
Knowing what I know now,
I probably would have chosen wrong.

Between You & Me

Between you and me, I'm sorry.
You're looking at someone
You thought you knew,
And wondering,
How'd we get here?

Between you and me, it's not your fault.
There are faults to find
In the air,
In their genes,
In the world,
But it's not
Your fault,
And it's not their fault.
There was just a perfect storm.

Between you and me, you're both going to suffer.
There will be moments
When they don't even know
Themselves,
And you,
You, will feel so far from them,
With mountains of secrets between.

When the anger or the sadness
Or the silence takes over
And they need you to stop
Reaching for them
Exactly as they need you
To reach for them,
Reach for them.

And between you and me, it's going to change
   things.
This will ruin family dinners, vacations,
And beautiful things, and
It will burden you,
To really help,
They will need you
To be hard on them.
And there will be guilt,
But be hard on them.

But between you and me,
Don't tell them you understand exactly
Because you went through something similar
When you were 18,
Which, maybe you did, but
Right now it seems
Like they are the only ones in the world.

And between you and me,
You're not going to "fix" them;
Therapy is not a 401k,
Where you put your feet up at 78,
And you do not buy
Medicine like a z-pack,
With a two-week max,
But know that they will have
Proud moments,
Good days and good years,
Happy tears,
They will just not be them
The way they were
Before—
It's just like any strength or flaw.

But between you and me,
One day there might be this moment,
When they find peace and know,
It doesn't scare them
Or send them running,
And they will get to be proud
Of themselves.
And one day
They'll find the strength
To help someone else,
Because they have more compassion now
Than anyone you have ever known.

And between you and me,
Their food is going to taste sweeter,
The view is going to look better,
The love is going to come harder
From their bones,
Because they have experienced the worst of it,
But they also get the best of it.
Their good days will be great
And their best moments
Will be such beautiful moments.

So between you and me,
I wouldn't wish this pain on anyone,
But I'd want the joy for everyone,
That relief when they make it
To the other side
And they know they will be okay.
And even when they are not,
They are not alone,
At war with themselves,
Because they have you
To go to hell and back

With them.

And between you and me,
Love isn't always enough,
But you're going to be
The reason they pull through,
And I know this much,
Because I'm writing
Right now,
From me to you

Safe Love

The hardest lesson to learn
Is that feeling safe
Is a privilege.
It's not a right,
Though it should be.

The feeling of safety can so easily be taken from us
In so many ways.

Our bodies and our minds are vulnerable
To the hands and choices of others.

I won't pretend to know
Your loss, your struggle, your trauma,
But don't pretend to know mine.

This is for all the people who thought I was cynical at 19
But also somehow too progressive for my own good,
As if my belief couldn't have been based on real life experiences,
And also on a little bit of hope that life could be different for other people.

They thought I was dreaming with my eyes open,
Well, if only they knew the nightmares I had anytime my eyes were closed.

This is for the ones that didn't really know me;
Sometimes I wanted you to know me.

Do you know what it's like to have been in a New York City classroom when the towers fell?
And then you have your family always pack a to-go bag from then on,
Just in case of emergencies?

Or what it's like to have a friend burden you
Before you are old enough to help them carry that burden?

Do you know what it's like to lay awake with a pool cue next to you,
Thinking of how you might protect the people closest to you
Because your own father wasn't who you thought he was,
And you knew if you closed your eyes,
You'd dream so vividly about losing the ones you loved
That you'd wake in terror, thinking that they were really gone?
And even when you did sleep, and did get up,
You would wake to see the fear in your mother's face?

Do you know what it's like for your therapist to try and ingrain in you, week after week,
That you are safe enough, you are safe enough, you are safe enough?

I think many of you do know what it's like;
I think too many of you know
What it's like to lose your mind to anxiety and obsession

And enter a place so dark you understand why
 people give up.

I think too many know what it's like
To feel unsafe in your own body, your own skin,
 your own mind,
In a constant fight with yourself.
And your therapist says, you're scared of hell?
Aren't you living it?
Aren't you already torturing yourself?
And you are,
In your mind,
As you curse your thoughts
And you berate your body that isn't working quite
 right
And you do pick at the scar on your face
And you hurt inside and out
And you think there is just so much pain,
Inside of you and in this world,
And it diminishes you.
And you diminish you.

And you get happy moments
In someone's arms,
Just lying in the sun,
Maybe on foreign streets because they make you
 feel safer than home,
But you also have to do the work.
And rebuilding is painful—a forever fight.
There's a reason we build defense mechanisms
To live behind.

I thought I was the exception, but now I think I'm
 the rule,

One person working to break the cycle of
 generations of trauma
So that I don't pass it on, so that maybe there's a
 better world for us in the future.

You think safety is a right until you don't feel safe
And then you can't go back
To the problems that you thought you had,
To the way you felt before.

I can never go back
To what my mind was like without OCD
And even if I could, it would probably make me
 uneasy.

But it, it exists in the same way most things in
 life do

It gets better
And it comes back
And it gets better
And it comes back
And it gets better

Dreams

When it got hard,
I used to say,
Where would I rather be—
At the start of a career
I'm in love with,
Even if I'm struggling,
Or at the other end of it,
Looking back at all I've done?
I want to be at the beginning,
I would always say,
Hustling, hoping, dreaming
Excited about the possibilities.

But then,
I experienced a little success
And it felt, so good.

Stay at the beginning too long and get restless,
But I don't want to have it all yet either.
I just want to be present for every step,
Like when, we put Front Row Seat out,
A song that meant a lot to us,
And I said, I hope it has the kind of quiet power in
    the world that it has in every room,
And I hope one day I do too.

When It Ends

I wonder how people will remember me.
I hope they remember that I was complicated,
That they talk about my kindness and intelligence and strength,
But also about how I was messy and human and sometimes dark.

I think about all the people I love gathering,
Each bringing together a fragment of me that they held,
Each piece different,
Each a part of me,
But even when put together,
Never quite the whole,
Because as much as I tried
I couldn't shake and share every speckle of dust
From every crevice in my mind.
I feel like I should now,
Unleash every thought I had
That I deemed to be bad,
That nearly shaped me at times
Into a person I was afraid to become.
I feel like I need to give the ones I will leave behind,
The whole picture
And shout, don't only look at the good of me,
I want to deserve the love and respect you lay me down with.

I say this now because even while alive, I know I am so loved.
But in preparing for my eventual death,

While I think about how those closest to me will
　　think of me then,
I worry,
That they will bathe me in light.

And yes, there are so many beautiful parts of me
But there are other parts too,
And alive I question—
Am I worthy of love?
Am I worthy of forgiveness?
From myself, from the universe?
Am I worthy of all the wonderful things and people
　　I have around me?

How ironic it will be
That when I finally have the answer
It will be too late
To unwrite this poem.

Most of all,
I just hope the ones I love know
That in the deepest, darkest parts of me
I still had the best of intentions
And I loved them so very much.

Presence

Don't rush;
Don't rush your life

Thank You

Thank you to my mother. I'm not perfect and neither was the path we walked, but we walked so much of it together. I treasure you and hope you see the large amounts of love you raised me with being put back into this world.

Thanks to my sister, Samantha, my best friend. (I write too many poems about her. She reads them all but emotions make her uncomfortable). Sammi, I look forward to this book destroying you emotionally.

My grandmother is no longer with us, but I come from a long line of strong women. She made some mistakes, but she also made some choices ahead of her time. I was lucky to know her.

I've had a majority of my other friends since the end of high school. I love them so much and we have been through some life together. I really appreciate them.

The reason these poems came together into a collection is because a good friend reminded me that poetry is my true foundation—it's who I am. It's where I can be most honest. She has changed my life over and over again. Thank you Maya.

Thank you to my Nashville family. I fucking love you guys. If I didn't, I would never have come back. D - thank you.

Thank you to Nick. Please know this list is not in order. You are my brother.

Thank you to my editor, Nicole Fegan. I could never have imagined an editor touching my poetry but you were the right person to trust.

Thank you to Marisa Paolillo for your beautiful artwork.

I also owe a moment of gratitude to the family members that are still a part of my life, the other grandparents who I barely knew but survived hell, Amanda, Stacey, and the strong women I have worked with that helped to raise me.

There are three English professors that changed my life. Matthew Burgess doesn't know it but he's part of the reason this collection exists.

Lastly but most certainly not least, thank you to the subjects of these poems. Some of you are still in my life and some of you aren't; but each and every one of you inspired me. I hope wherever you are, you are happy.

To all the people that mean so much to me, I love you all deeply. There will never be enough words to summarize my gratitude but I will try anyway; thank you.

I hope I captured just a little bit of the magical essence of each of you.